TRAVELLING WILD
TPB09-5

SAILING THE CARIBBEAN ISLANDS

Sonya Newland

WAYLAND
www.waylandbooks.co.uk

First published in Great Britain in 2016
by Wayland

Copyright © Wayland, 2016

ISBN: 978 0 7502 9865 0
10 9 8 7 6 5 4 3 2 1

MIX
Paper from
responsible sources
FSC® C104740

Wayland
An imprint of
Hachette Children's Group
Part of Hodder & Stoughton
Carmelite House
50 Victoria Embankment
London EC4Y 0DZ

An Hachette UK Company
www.hachette.co.uk

www.hachettechildrens.co.uk

A catalogue for this title is available
from the British Library

Printed and bound in China

Produced for Wayland by
White-Thomson Publishing Ltd
www.wtpub.co.uk

Author: Sonya Newland
Designer: Rocket Design (East Anglia) Ltd
Picture researcher: Izzi Howell
Map: Stefan Chabluk
Wayland editor: Elizabeth Brent

Picture credits:
P5 Christian Wheatley/iStock;
P6 Matthew Connolly/Shutterstock;
P7 frantisekhojdysz/Shutterstock;
P8 National Geographic Creative/Alamy;
P9T Rich Carey/Shutterstock; P9B Gerardo
Borbolla/Shutterstock; P10 WaterFrame/
Alamy; P11T WaterFrame/Shutterstock;
P11B Gudkov Andrey/Shutterstock;
P12 Yann Hubert/Shutterstock; P13T
Ethan Daniels/Shutterstock; P13B
dean bertoncelj/Shutterstock; P14
InsectWorld/Shutterstock; P15T Jason
Patrick Ross/Shutterstock; p15b Doug
Perrine/Nature Picture Library/Corbis;
P16 Anna Jedynak/Shutterstock; P17T
Juanmonino/IStock; P17B holbox/
Shutterstock; P18 Global_Pics/
Shutterstock; P19T Vilainecrevette/
Shutterstock; P19B Vilainecrevette/
Shutterstock; P20 old apple/Shutterstock;
p21T MichaelStubblefield/iStock; P21B
holbox/Shutterstock; P22 Ozphotoguy/
Shutterstock; P23T Peeter Viisimaa/
iStock; P23B Kkulikov/Shutterstock;
P24 Kenneth Wiedemann/iStock;
P25 Ralph White/Corbis; P26
johnandersonphoto/iStock; P27T Robert
Harding/Alamy; P27B cdascher/iStock;
P28T Kamira/Shutterstock; P28B
Konstantin Aksenov/Shutterstock;
P29 Sean Pavone/Shutterstock.

CONTENTS

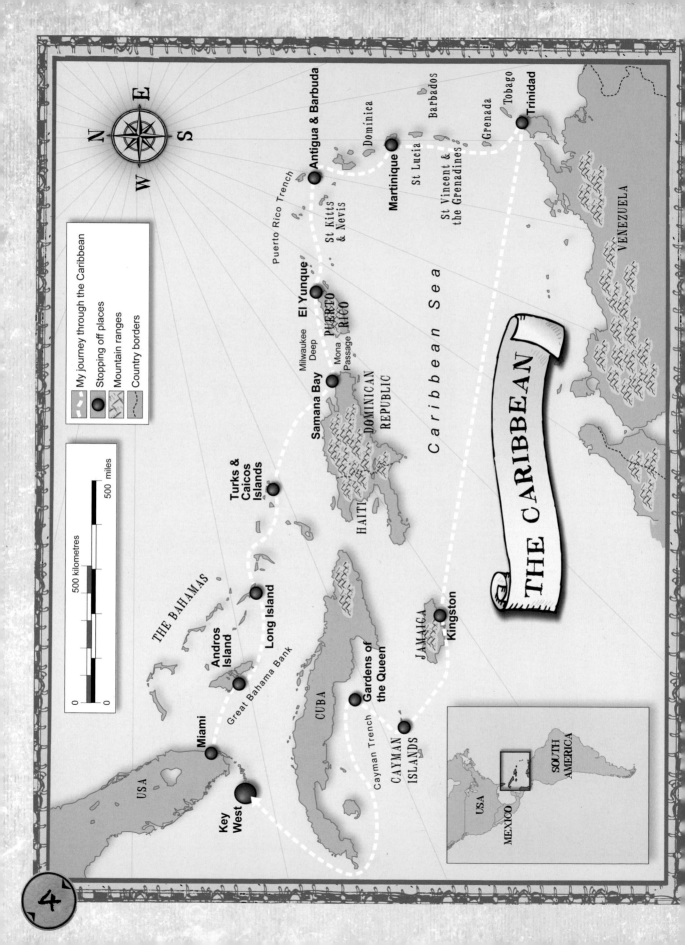

THE CARIBBEAN

My journey through the Caribbean
Stopping off places
Mountain ranges
Country borders

500 kilometres
500 miles

N
E
S
W

USA

THE BAHAMAS

Miami

Key West

Andros Island

Long Island

Great Bahama Bank

CUBA

Gardens of the Queen

Cayman Trench

CAYMAN ISLANDS

JAMAICA

Kingston

Turks & Caicos Islands

HAITI

DOMINICAN REPUBLIC

Samana Bay

Mona Passage

Milwaukee Deep

PUERTO RICO

El Yunque

Puerto Rico Trench

St Kitts & Nevis

Antigua & Barbuda

Dominica

Martinique

St Lucia

Barbados

St Vincent & the Grenadines

Grenada

Tobago

Trinidad

Caribbean Sea

VENEZUELA

USA

MEXICO

SOUTH AMERICA

4

THE CARIBBEAN SEA

Preparing for the trip

I can't believe I'm finally setting off on my great adventure! Tomorrow I leave for Florida in the United States, and from there I'll be setting sail around the Caribbean Sea. The pictures make the Caribbean seem like a place of endless sunshine and sandy beaches, but I know there are going to be dangers along the way – including sharks and other deadly creatures. But I've been preparing for weeks and now I can't wait to set sail!

Islands in the sea

The region known as the Caribbean covers the 2.7 million square km of the Caribbean Sea and more than 7,000 islands within it. There are two main island groups – the Greater Antilles in the northern part, which includes most of the larger islands, and the Lesser Antilles in the south. These are further divided into three groups: the Leeward Islands, the Windward Islands and the Leeward Antilles. Many of the islands are overseas territories of other countries, but 13 of them are independent countries.

When to sail

I don't want to get caught in one of the hurricanes that sweep this part of the world from June to November, so I've planned my journey to begin in February. This is the middle of the dry season so hopefully it will be warm and sunny, with no rough seas! It's also the best time to see some of the marine wildlife I'm hoping to encounter on my travels.

Equipment

I've decided to bring along the following:

- waterproof clothing
- life jacket
- snorkelling gear
- rubber shoes
- scuba gear
- dive light
- dive knife
- map and compass
- binoculars
- medical kit including seasickness pills
- sun cream

SHARKS OF THE SHALLOW SEAS

8 February
Miami to Andros Island

I set sail a couple of days ago from the sunny city of Miami, in the USA, heading towards Andros Island in the Bahamas. Things have started well – the sea is calm and there's not a cloud in the sky. I'd love to take a dip in the ocean to cool off, but the water here is teeming with sharks so I think I'll stay on board for now!

The Bahamas

Lying in the Atlantic Ocean to the south-east of Florida, the Bahamas are a group of around 700 islands. Only 26 of them are inhabited and Andros Island is the largest of these. The name Bahamas means 'shallow seas' and I can see why: stretching for 530 km between here and Cuba is the Great Bahama Bank – a massive limestone platform beneath the water. The sea here is only 25 m at its deepest.

Types of shark

More than 40 species of shark can be found around the Bahamas, attracted by the warm, clear waters.

• Tiger sharks are the most dangerous sharks in the world after great white sharks. They can grow up to 6 m long, and will eat almost anything!

• Bull sharks aren't the biggest sharks, but they are among the deadliest, and they will attack humans. You can spot a bull shark by its thick body, blunt snout and long fins on the sides of its body.

• Blacktip reef sharks are common in the Caribbean, but they are shy and pose no threat to humans. They can be identified by the black marking on the tip of the dorsal fin on their backs.

• Nurse sharks are among the biggest and heaviest species in the Caribbean, and adults can weigh up to 350 kg. These sharks rest in the day and hunt at night.

Shark attack!

Not all sharks are dangerous, but if you find yourself in the water with one, keep as still as you can – most of them will simply swim away. If you are unlucky enough to be attacked by a shark, hit and kick it as hard as you can, aiming for the eyes and the gills.

Be smart, survive!

Sharks and other sea creatures will be attracted to rubbish. To avoid the waters around your boat filling up with sharp-toothed sharks, don't throw anything overboard. Always dispose of your waste responsibly on land.

UNDERWATER WORLD

12 February
Andros Island to
Long Island, the Bahamas

I've just crossed the Tropic of Cancer
and dropped anchor off the coast
of Long Island. It's really beautiful
here. Looking to the shore I can see
dramatic cliffs rising above empty
white-sand beaches. But I've actually
stopped in this spot to explore a
different type of landscape – I'm
finally about to dive into the amazing
underwater world.

Dean's Blue Hole

The Bahamas are famous for their
'blue holes'. These are depressions, or
sinkholes, in the sea, where the water
is so deep that it looks much darker
than the surrounding water. Dean's
Blue Hole, near Long Island, is the
deepest saltwater blue hole in the
world with an entrance below sea level.
One of the most famous blue holes,
the 300–m–wide Great Blue Hole, can
be found on the other side of the
Caribbean, off the coast of Belize.

8

Seagrass

Seagrass is not actually grass, but flowering plants that carpet the sea bed in many shallow coastal lagoons and estuaries in the Caribbean. These underwater meadows are home to hundreds of species of sea creatures, including fish, sea urchins, turtles and strange-looking marine mammals called dugongs. These important underwater ecosystems are under threat from water pollution and coastal development in the Caribbean.

There are many places in the Caribbean where divers can explore the remains of ships that have sunk beneath the waves. The Royal Navy ship *Conqueror* sank in 1855 near the island of Rum Cay, not far from Long Island. The site of the wreck is now an underwater museum. The wreck of the *Rhone*, which sank in a hurricane in the British Virgin Islands in 1867, is one of the most eerie and dramatic dive sites in the Caribbean.

Be smart, survive!

Underwater shipwrecks are fascinating, but they can also be dangerous for divers. Always go slowly and carefully when wreck diving, and try not to bump into anything - this could damage your equipment as well as the wreck. Use a guideline if you go inside the wreck, and make sure your dive light is in full working order before you enter!

MANGROVE FORESTS

22 February
Long Island to the Turks and Caicos Islands

I've stopped at the Turks and Caicos Islands, a British overseas territory, because I want to explore the mangroves here – an important habitat for coastal plants and animals in the Caribbean. I've had a brilliant day travelling in a kayak through the shallow waters, turtle-spotting and learning about this vital but threatened ecosystem.

The mangrove ecosystem

Mangroves are swampy areas of trees and shrubs that grow in places frequently flooded by the tides, such as lagoons and estuaries. They are important because they protect the coast from storms. They also filter pollutants from the water that would otherwise end up harming the coral reefs and marine wildlife along the coast. But the mangroves are under threat, as large areas are being cut down to make way for tourist developments and so that people can use the wood.

Red and black

Two main types of mangroves grow in the Caribbean — red and black. The red mangroves are the tallest; some of them can grow to 25 m. They get their name from the reddish-coloured wood of their trunks. Black mangroves are shorter, growing to around 20 m, and are covered in dark, scaly bark. The roots of both types can be seen beneath the water.

Be smart, survive!

In most parts of the mangrove forests the water is shallow enough to wade through. It's better to travel by kayak or paddleboard, but if you want to go wandering on foot, be sure to wear rubber shoes so your feet don't get cut on sharp rocks or stones on the sea bed or on the mangrove roots.

Mangrove wildlife

Mangroves are home to all sorts of animals. They are particularly important to sea turtles, which come here for food and to give birth to their young. Conservationists are working to protect the turtles and their environment on the Turks and Caicos Islands. The mangroves also function as nurseries for many fish species, which give birth to their young in these protected waters. Keeping the mangroves safe from development means that there will be plenty of fish to be caught and sold.

Mangroves are alive with birds as well as animals, including flamingos and parrots.

WHALES AND DOLPHINS

27 February
The Turks and Caicos Islands to Samana Bay, the Dominican Republic

This has to be one of the highlights of my trip! As I was sailing out from the Turks and Caicos Islands, I saw a pod of whales travelling through the Turks Island Passage, heading from the Atlantic Ocean into the Caribbean. The sight of these magnificent creatures leaping in the water near my boat made me want to find out more about them. I decided to see where they were heading ...

Whale migration

The whales I'm following are North Atlantic humpbacks. Every year, between February and April, these gentle giants migrate up to 25,000 km to the warm waters of the Caribbean Sea off the coast of the Dominican Republic. They come here to give birth to their young. In the late spring, they'll be off again to the cooler waters of the North Atlantic, where food is more plentiful.

Be smart, survive!

Diving is a great way to get close to underwater wildlife, but it can be dangerous. Follow these tips to stay safe:

1 Check your scuba equipment carefully before you get in the water to make sure it's all working as it should.

2 Always dive with a buddy and stay in sight of each other at all times.

3 Keep a constant eye on the amount of air you have left.

4 Don't venture too far from your boat - remember, if you run out of air far away, you'll have to swim back.

5 Don't touch plants, coral or creatures.

Marine mammals

Humpbacks aren't the only whales in the Caribbean waters. Pilot whales, sperm whales and beaked whales are among several species that use the central Caribbean as their migratory route each year. In more southern parts, you can spot sperm whales and pygmy right whales all year round. Other marine mammals, such as spotted and bottlenose dolphins, can also be seen gliding through the clear Caribbean waters.

Spotted dolphins can be identified by their speckled bodies.

Tourism

The Dominican Republic is the most popular tourist destination in the Caribbean, and its capital, Santo Domingo, is the largest city in the region. Thousands of visitors come here to go on whale-watching trips. This kind of activity is important to the economy, but unfortunately it also has a negative effect. Natural habitats have been turned into tourist resorts, and coastal development has resulted in increased pollution, which is harming the marine environment.

NATURAL WONDERS

3 March
Samana Bay to El Yunque, Puerto Rico

My journey through the Mona Passage wasn't the most pleasant experience – it was all I could do to stop myself being seasick in those choppy waters! But it was worth it to get to Puerto Rico, where I've been exploring the tropical rainforest El Yunque. The mountains and trees here offer a very different Caribbean landscape from the sand and sea I've experienced so far. It's as if I've wandered into another world.

Mona Passage

The Mona Passage is a 130-km-wide strait between the Dominican Republic and Puerto Rico. This is where the waters of the Atlantic Ocean and the Caribbean Sea meet, and it runs along the edge of the Milwaukee Deep – the deepest point in the Atlantic Ocean. The long sandbanks make the sea dangerously shallow in places, so this is a particularly risky route for sailors.

Rough seas

You never know what kind of conditions you're going to encounter on the open sea, so it's best to be prepared for the worst. Always wear a life jacket on a boat, even in calm weather. Before you set sail, practise emergency procedures such as how to launch your life raft. During your trip, make regular checks of it and other emergency equipment, such as life buoys, to make sure they won't let you down in your moment of need!

GET OUT ALIVE!!

El Yunque

The rainforest of El Yunque stretches across 115 square km of north-east Puerto Rico, around the Luquillo Mountains. It rains all year round, so the forest is alive with plants and animals, waterfalls and fast-flowing rivers. More than 50 different types of orchid grow here, as well as giant ferns and hanging vines called lianas, which wrap themselves around the trees.

Bio Bay

While I'm in here, I take the opportunity to see another amazing natural sight, at Bioluminescent Bay on the tiny nearby island of Vieques. As night descends, the water in the bay glows with an eerie blue-green light. This is caused by micro-organisms called dinoflagellates. These strange creatures — half plant, half animal — are bioluminescent, which means that chemical reactions in their bodies make light. Billions of dinoflagellates live in the water here, bringing it to life after dark.

10 March
El Yunque to Antigua and Barbuda

My journey from Puerto Rico has taken me on a winding route around some of the northern Leeward Islands. This is an arc of islands marking the boundary between the Caribbean and the western Atlantic. I'm spending a couple of days on the twin islands of Antigua and Barbuda. This little country lives up to its nickname of 'the land of 365 beaches', and I'm enjoying the pleasant cooling breezes of the trade winds.

The Caribbean climate

Most of the Caribbean has a tropical climate, which means that it's warm all year round. Temperatures average around 24°C to 32°C, but can vary quite a lot depending on which island you're on and where on an island you are! It can be much cooler in the mountainous regions of islands such as Jamaica and the Dominican Republic than it is further south. Most parts of the Caribbean have wet and dry seasons, with the wet season running from June to November and the dry season from December to May.

Trade winds are steady winds that blow from east to west towards the Equator in earth's tropical zones. They are caused by hot air rising at the Equator and being replaced by cooler air coming in from the north and south. These winds were named by sailors in the days when trade ships made long journeys westwards, helped along by the winds behind them. The trade winds blow all the time across the Caribbean Sea, but they are strongest in December and January.

Hurricanes

Hurricanes are massive storms or spiralling winds that build up over open seas. They form in tropical regions north and south of the Equator. Although they don't often occur in southern parts of the Caribbean, they are common further north. Hurricane season is from the beginning of June to the end of November, but these huge storms have been known to batter Caribbean coastlines outside these months, too.

Hurricane havoc

Hurricanes can be huge – some of them are nearly 1,000 km across – and winds can be up to 300 km/h. If hurricanes hit a coastline, they can tear up trees, destroy buildings and cause huge waves to come crashing on to shore, flooding streets and houses. If you're travelling in an area where hurricanes occur, make sure you have plenty of emergency supplies such as bottled water and a medical kit so you can outlast the storm.

GET OUT ALIVE !!

17

COLOURFUL FISH

15 March
Antigua and Barbuda
to Martinique

From Antigua and Barbuda I headed
south around Guadeloupe and past
Dominica - the first of the Windward
Islands. As I stopped near the French
island of Martinique, shoals of colourful
fish surrounded the boat, so I decided
to go snorkelling to take a closer look.
I was having a wonderful time swimming
amongst them, until I came face to face
with one of the scariest-looking fish I've
ever seen - a barracuda!

Barracuda

These fearsome predators of the
underwater world can grow to nearly
2 m long, and are usually seen alone,
hunting shoals of fish. When they go
for the attack they can move
incredibly fast — up to 50 km/h.
Barracudas swim with their
mouth open, revealing rows of
terrifying teeth. But although this gives
them a frightening appearance, it is
actually just how the fish pushes water
through its gills.

Diversity of fish

More than 1,000 species of fish live in the Caribbean Sea, from huge reef sharks to tiny gobies.

• Angelfish and butterflyfish are some of the most colourful in the Caribbean. These inquisitive fish are usually patterned with wide or narrow stripes or speckles, with fins of contrasting colours.

• Parrotfish are another brilliantly colourful inhabitant of these waters. These unusual fish have beaks rather than teeth, which they use to scrape algae from coral.

• Among the larger fish that live in the Caribbean are various species of grouper. Some of these grow up to 0.6 m long and can be identified by the spines on their back above the dorsal fin.

Be smart, survive!

Snorkelling is one of the best ways to experience the underwater world of the Caribbean, but you should ensure you snorkel safely. Always stay with a partner and make sure you can see each other at all times. Never go too far from the boat or the shore in case you get tired. It helps to wear a flotation device such as a snorkelling vest, too.

Barracuda attack!

Barracudas will not usually attack divers, but there are reported cases of barracudas showing aggressive behaviour towards humans, even if they're not provoked. And a bite from those sharp teeth is something to be avoided at all costs! The best thing to do if a barracuda gets too close to you is to back away slowly, without making any sudden movements.

GET OUT ALIVE !!

LAND AND SEA BIRDS

22 March
Martinique to Trinidad and Tobago

I've finally reached the southernmost point on my journey – the Windward Islands of Trinidad and Tobago. I wanted to stop here because I've heard that this is a great place for bird-watching, so I headed to a bird sanctuary on Trinidad. I hadn't expected to see such an amazing variety of bird life in one place!

Birds on land

Many bird species on the Windward Islands are typical of the tropical regions of nearby South America, including a wide variety of colourful parrots and talkative toucans. Small yellow-and-black bananaquits and kiskadees, kingbirds and tanagers of all different colours are a common sight in gardens across the Caribbean.

Bird migration

There are around 500 species of bird native to the twin islands of Trinidad and Tobago. This is a huge number for such a small country (together the two islands cover only about 5,000 square km). During the northern winter, many non-native species can be spotted here too, because the islands are on the route of birds migrating from North America. It really is a bird-watcher's paradise!

The scarlet ibis is the national bird of Trinidad and Tobago.

Be smart, survive!

Birds are easily scared by noise and movement, especially when they are nesting. If you scare away an adult, they may leave the nest, exposing the eggs or chicks to predators. Always watch nesting birds from a distance, using binoculars. Never try to touch the birds or their chicks. If you're going ashore from a boat to do some bird-watching, try to land and launch your boat far enough from the birds to avoid scaring them.

Birds at sea

Bird-watching isn't just something you can do on land in the Caribbean: the skies above the sea are filled with ocean-going birds such as tropic birds and boobies. The male magnificent frigatebird is one of the easiest to spot because of its vivid red chest, which it swells up when it's trying to attract a mate. Sea birds like these swoop low over the surface of the water and dive to catch their fish prey.

CARIBBEAN CULTURE

12 April
Trinidad to Kingston, Jamaica

Despite the trade winds at my back, it was a long journey across the open sea to my next stop on land. Because several countries have conquered different parts of the Caribbean for hundreds of years, each island has its own distinct style. I was keen to reach Kingston, the lively, colourful capital of Jamaica, and experience the culture there.

Every island in the Caribbean has its own unique atmosphere, and a huge range of customs and traditions can be seen across the region. Countries such as Britain, France and Spain have all affected the lifestyles and culture of the Caribbean islanders, but influences from Africa and the Americas are also evident. The islanders speak a variety of languages, including creoles and patois — types of speech that mix several languages.

Jamaica

English is the official language of Jamaica, because the island was conquered by Britain in the seventeenth century. However, many Jamaicans are of African descent, as the British brought slaves from Africa to work on the sugar plantations here. Sugar is still an important industry on the island.

The Blue Mountains

While I'm here I've decided to do a bit of exploring on foot, so I'm off hiking in the Blue Mountains, home of the famous Blue Mountain coffee plantation. From high up here, the views across the Caribbean are spectacular. When the mists clear, it's possible to see all the way across to Cuba, more than 200 km away.

Be smart, survive!

Seasickness can be a sailor's curse. If you're spending a long time on the water, try the following tips to avoid getting seasick:

- Watch a fixed point on the boat or keep your eyes on the horizon.
- Spend time above board in the fresh air rather than below deck.
- Avoid foods that have strong smells or flavours.
- Take seasickness pills!

Overboard!

If you find yourself alone in the water and in need of rescue, don't thrash around, as this will cause you to keep sinking and will use up your energy. Your body is naturally buoyant and will keep you on the surface. Try to float on your back with your arms and legs spread wide, keeping your face out of the water, until help arrives.

THE CAYMAN TRENCH

20 April
Kingston to the Cayman Islands

I set sail again, cruising round the southern and western coasts of Jamaica and back out into the open sea towards the Cayman Islands. This British overseas territory is made up of three islands, and I've disembarked on the largest, Grand Cayman. The vibe here is very different from Jamaica. This island is a centre of finance, and the wealth is evident in the glamorous resorts.

Deep-sea trenches

To reach the Cayman Islands, I sailed right over the Cayman Trench. This deep-sea trench starts in the Windward Passage, the strip of sea between Haiti and Cuba, and stretches almost to Guatemala in the west. Trenches like this usually form at the boundary of two of the earth's tectonic plates. Here, the North American plate meets the Caribbean plate. Underwater earthquakes are quite common in these areas, caused by the slowly moving plates.

Sea itch

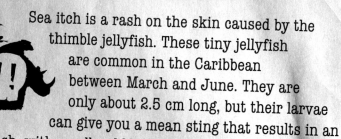

Sea itch is a rash on the skin caused by the thimble jellyfish. These tiny jellyfish are common in the Caribbean between March and June. They are only about 2.5 cm long, but their larvae can give you a mean sting that results in an uncomfortable rash, with small red blisters, that can last for several days. The larvae are so small that they get under swimsuits and wetsuits. If you find you've been stung, remove your bathing gear and shower in clean sea water – fresh water will make the rash worse.

Be smart, survive!

Sunburn and heatstroke are real dangers here in the Caribbean, especially at sea. I try to avoid being out in the midday heat, and whenever I'm in the sunshine I drink plenty of water to keep hydrated. I also make sure I'm covered in a high-factor sun cream and I always wear a hat when I'm on deck.

Deep-sea vents

One part of the Cayman Trench is the deepest point in the Caribbean Sea – sinking an incredible 7,686 m into the earth. But there is activity even deeper beneath the surface here. Deep—sea vents are thin cracks in the surface of the earth, from which boiling water and smoke escape. The deep—sea vents in the Cayman Trench are the deepest and the hottest in the world. Some of them go as far as 5 km into the earth.

REEF LIFE

25 April
Cayman Islands to Cuba

I've been in the Caribbean for two and a half months but I haven't properly explored one of the area's most beautiful and important ecosystems - coral reefs. Across the Caribbean Sea are more than 50,000 square km of reefs (that's about nine per cent of the world's total), and one of the greatest is the Gardens of the Queen, here off the coast of Cuba.

Coral reefs

Coral reefs are underwater structures made of calcium carbonate produced by tiny creatures called polyps. Reefs are found in warm, shallow seas close to coastlines, so the Caribbean provides the perfect conditions for them to grow. The reefs themselves are a vital habitat for hundreds of species of plants, fish and other sea creatures. There are several long reefs in the Caribbean, including the second—largest in the world — the Belize Barrier Reef — and the Gardens of the Queen.

Be smart, survive!

Take care around coral reefs. It's important to avoid damaging the delicate coral, but bear in mind that it can also harm you. Always wear a wetsuit in areas where there is coral and try to avoid coming into contact with it. If you get cut or scratched by coral, wash the area thoroughly with a saline solution.

Environmental issues

The amount of coral in the Caribbean has declined dramatically in recent years. Tourists who go diving and snorkelling in the sea often do not take as much care as they should and cause irreversible damage to the reef system. There are now great efforts being made to protect the coral that remains, by educating people about treating it with respect, and by creating special protected areas such as the Gardens of the Queen.

The Gardens of the Queen

The Gardens of the Queen is a maritime reserve lying about 100 km off the coast of Cuba. Within this amazing underwater world is a 50-km-long barrier reef. Here you can see the whole ecosystem at work, including hunting predators such as sharks and groupers. It is also possible to see coral spawning in August, when the coral all release their eggs and sperm in a great cloud that rises to the surface and lingers there for days.

JOURNEY'S END

14 May
Cuba to Key West, Florida

My journey is over, and it's ended just in time. The wet season will soon be here and I'll be glad not to be on my boat during a hurricane! I'm sitting in the sunshine at Key West in Florida – the southernmost point of the United States mainland. As I stare out over the brilliant blue of the ocean, I think of all the things I've seen in the past few months and what an amazing experience this has been.

Cuba

The last leg of my journey took me round the coast of much of Cuba. At 110,000 square km and with a population of around 11 million, this is the largest island in the Caribbean Sea. Exploring the capital, Havana, gives an insight into its history. Cuba was once a colony of Spain, and although it is now an independent country, the Spanish influence is evident everywhere. Spanish is still the official language and much of the architecture in Havana and elsewhere is in the Spanish colonial style.

Be smart, survive!

The Caribbean is one of the most popular tourist destinations in the world, but tourism is having a negative effect on the natural environment, both on the islands and in the Caribbean Sea. Ecotourism is one way to make sure that you visit this region without contributing to that damage, and there are now many tour operators offering holidays that help conserve the Caribbean ecosystems.

Caribbean conservation

On my long journey, I've learnt that the Caribbean is a beautiful and diverse part of the world. It's a shame that some of the most important habitats here are under threat from coastal development, pollution and the effects of tourism on features such as the coral reefs. The people of the Caribbean value these natural environments and there are many conservation efforts in place. Hopefully they will continue to preserve this amazing place and its wildlife — those that live on land and beneath the sea.

GLOSSARY

algae A type of plant that includes seaweed.

bioluminescent Living creatures that produce their own light through chemical reactions within them.

colony When a country has been taken over by another country.

conservationist A person or organisation that campaigns or acts for the protection of the natural environment.

deep-sea trench A long, steep-sided depression in the earth's crust at the bottom of the ocean.

depression A large dip in the ground.

dorsal fin The fin on the back of sea creatures such as sharks and dolphins.

economy The system of how money is made and used in a particular country or region.

ecosystem All the plants and animals in a particular environment.

ecotourism Tourism that aims to support conservation efforts in threatened natural environments.

estuary The mouth of a river, where it flows into the sea.

hydrated Having enough water.

inhabited Lived in.

kayak A type of canoe made of a light frame with a watertight covering and a small opening at the top to sit in.

lagoon An area of saltwater separated from the sea by a strip of land.

larvae A young form of an insect and some other creatures that looks a bit like a worm.

limestone A type of hard rock.

marine Of or found in the sea.

micro-organism A tiny creature that is too small to see with the naked eye.

migrate To move from one region to another in different seasons.

overseas territories Countries that are ruled by another country.

pod A social group of whales.

pollutants Substances such as chemicals and rubbish that can be harmful to the environment.

polyp A creature with a column-shaped body, topped by a mouth surrounded by a ring of tentacles; the animals that create coral reefs are polyps.

predator An animal that hunts other animals for food.

prey An animal that is hunted by other animals for food.

rainforest A dense forest, rich in plant and animal life, with consistently heavy rainfall, usually found in tropical areas.

saline solution A saltwater solution used to clean wounds.

shoal Lots of fish swimming together.

sinkhole A large hole in the ground created by water wearing away rock.

strait A narrow strip of water that connects two seas or other large bodies of water.

tectonic plates Giant pieces of the earth's crust that move around very slowly.

Tropic of Cancer The imaginary line around the earth halfway between the North Pole and the Equator.

INDEX & FURTHER INFORMATION

Books

Caribbean (A World of Food) by Jen Green (Franklin Watts, 2016)
Cuba (Countries Around the World) by Frank Collins (Raintree, 2012)
Caribbean (Look at Countries) by Jillian Powell (Franklin Watts, 2010)
St Lucia: the Land and the People by Daniel Gilpin (Wayland, 2013)

Websites

http://www.activecaribbean.com/caribbean_wildlife.html
http://wwf.panda.org/what_we_do/endangered_species/marine_turtles/lac_marine_turtle_programme/projects/hawksbill_caribbean_english/caribbean_sea/

TRAVELLING
WILD
TPB09-5

OTHER TITLES IN THE TRAVELLING WILD SERIES

9780750285841

9780750298612

9780750298643

9780750298650

9780750283052

9780750283236

9780750283243

9780750283250